Koalas, Kites and Kangaroos

An Australian Alphabet Book

Koalas, kites and kangaroos,
Penguins and possums and pelicans too.
Worm-eating wagtails and wombats at play,
Surf-riding seals on a hot summer's day.
Rabbits on roller-skates, lizards on land,
Card-playing crocodiles, shells on the sand.
Turn over the pages and take a close look
At this wonderful, colourful ALPHABET BOOK!

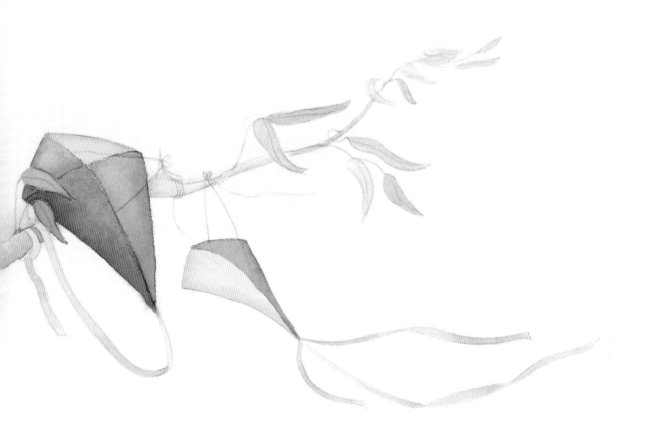

Aa

ant

apple

apron

Ayers Rock

Bb

ball

bicycle

bonnet

bowl

butterfly

Cc

cap

cards

claws

cockatoo

crocodile

Dd

dragonfly

drink

duck

Ee

egg

emu

eye

Ff

fish

flies

footprints

frog

Gg

glasses

glove

goanna

golf clubs

grasshopper

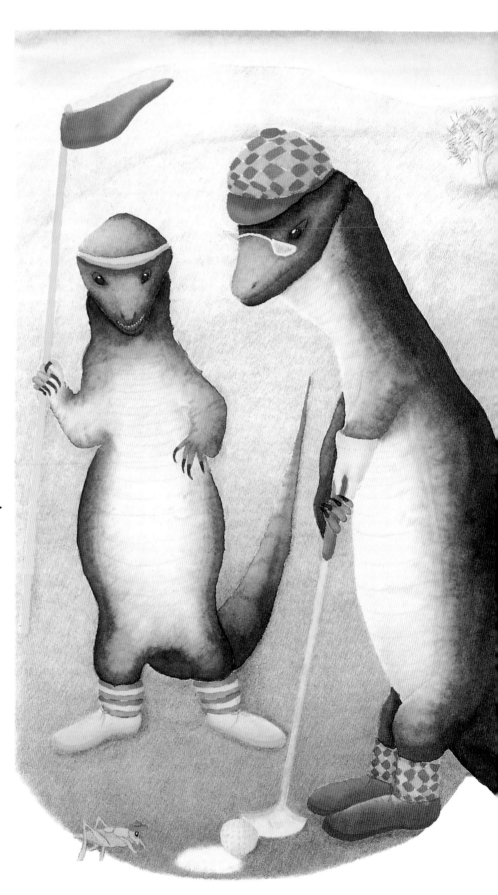

Hh

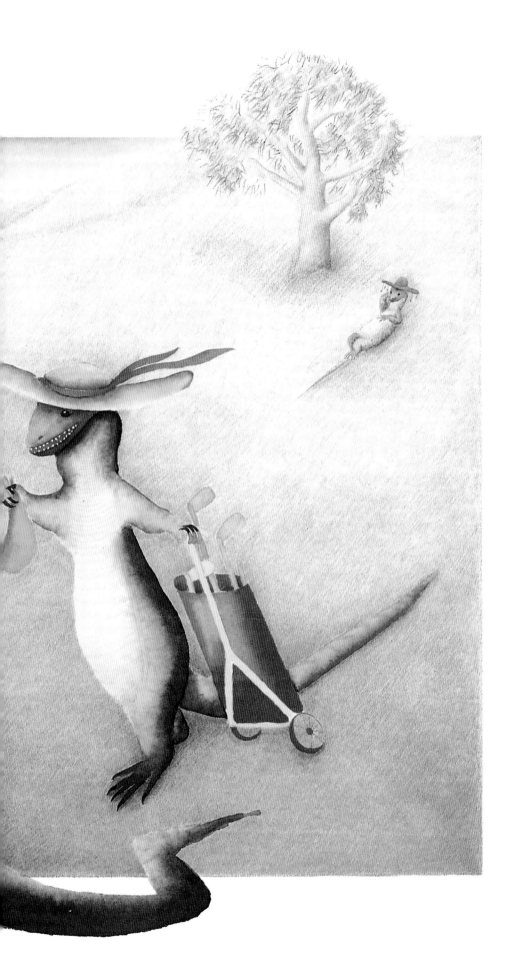

handkerchief

hat

headband

hill

hole

Ii

ice

icecream

invitation

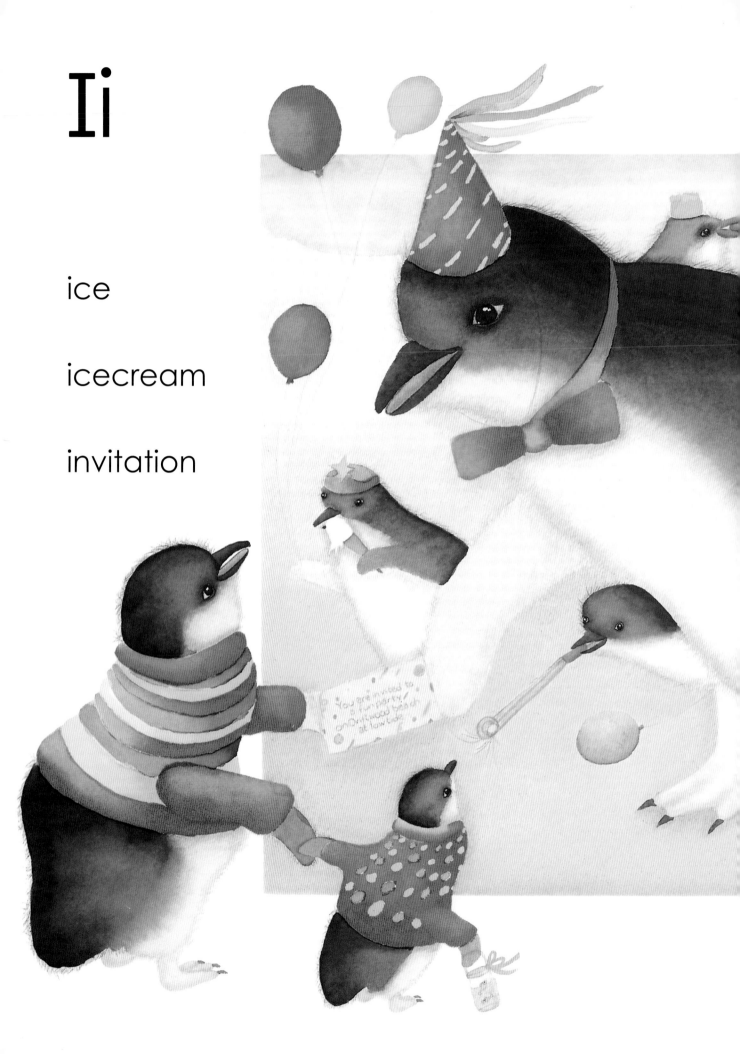

Jj

jacket

jar

jelly

jug

jumper

Kk

kangaroo

kite

koala

kookaburra

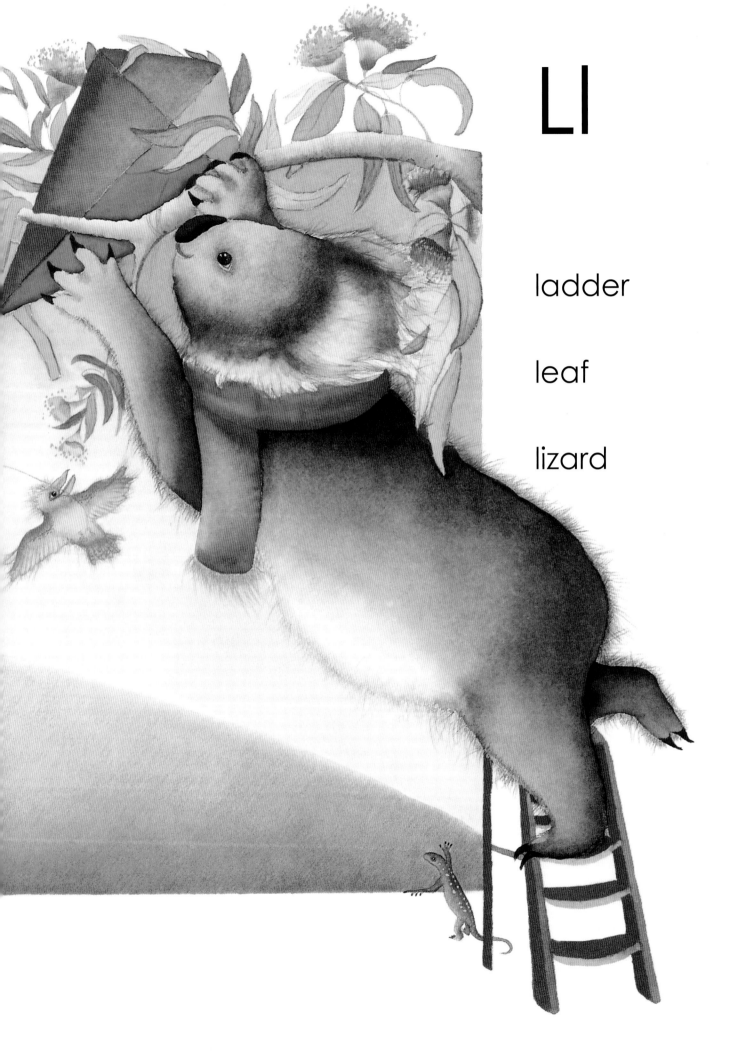

Ll

ladder

leaf

lizard

Mm

magpie

milk

moon

mouse

mug

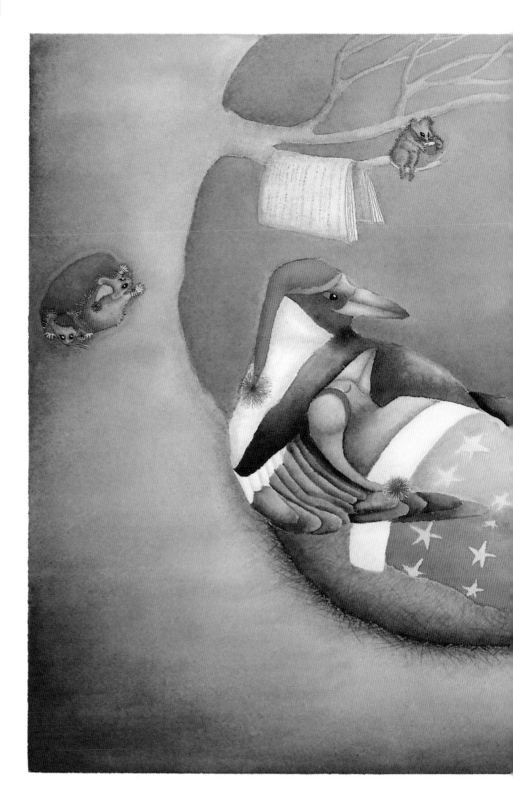

Nn

newspaper

nightcap

nuts

Oo

olives

orange

owl

Pp

parrot

pear

peel

plum

possum

Qq

queue

quill

quilt

Rr

rabbit

red

ribbon

roller-skates

rose

Ss

sandcastle

seagull

seal

snorkel

surfboard

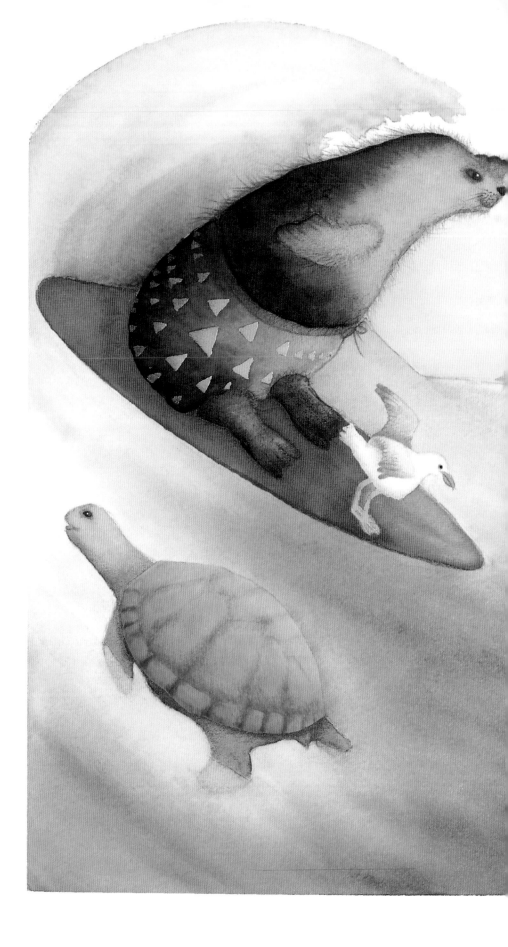

Tt

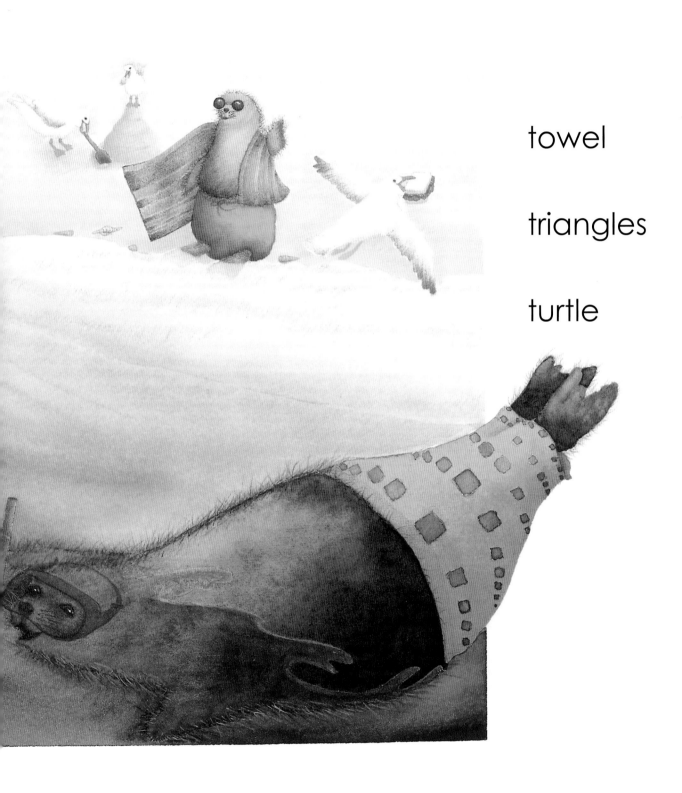

towel

triangles

turtle

Uu

umbrella

underneath

upturned

Vv

vegemite

vegetable

violin

Ww

wagtail

water

wheelbarrow

wombat

worm

Xx

box

fox

exit

Yy

yak

yellow

yoyo

Zz

zoo

zebra

zigzag

zoo keeper

Koalas, kites and kangaroos,
We've listed here more words for you.
They're found in the pictures,
So take a close look
For the things you have missed
In this ALPHABET BOOK!

Aa	anteater	**Pp**	peach
Bb	baby		peeler
	bib	**Qq**	quarter to twelve
	bird	**Rr**	rug
	bottle	**Ss**	sand
Cc	cushion		sandwich
Dd	deck of cards		sea
Ee	-		shells
Ff	feet		spade
Gg	golf ball		squares
	gum tree		starfish
Hh	head		sunglasses
Ii	ice cube		surf
Jj	-	**Tt**	tide
Kk	-	**Uu**	-
Ll	log	**Vv**	-
Mm	mushroom	**Ww**	watering can
Nn	nest		watermelon
	night		wellington boots
Oo	-	**Xx**	-
		Yy	-
		Zz	zoo helper
			zoo ticket

First published 1985 by Childerset Publishers, Cairns, Australia
First published in paperback 1990
Reprinted 1991, 1992, 1993, 1996, 1999
Text copyright © David Ridyard 1985
Illustrations copyright © Doreen Gristwood 1985

This edition published by Scholastic Australia in 2013.

National Library of Australia Cataloguing-in-Publication entry

Author: Ridyard, David, 1942- author.
Title: Koalas, kites and kangaroos / David Ridyard, illustrated by Doreen Gristwood.
ISBN: 978 174283 872 4. (pbk.)
Target Audience: For pre-school age children.
Subjects: English language--Alphabet--Juvenile literature.
Other Authors/Contributors: Gristwood, Doreen, 1959- illustrator.
Dewey Number: 421.1